THE ART OF DRAWING
MANGA™

GIRLS
&1BOYS

Author: Max Marlborough has been passionate about graphic design and manga from an early age and works as a freelance author, illustrator and designer of art guides for readers of all ages.

Artist: David Antram studied at Eastbourne College of Art and then worked in advertising for fifteen years before becoming a full-time artist. He has since illustrated many popular information books for children and young adults, including more than 60 titles in the bestselling *You Wouldn't Want To Be* series.

Additional artwork: Shutterstock

Published in Great Britain in MMXIX by Book House, an imprint of **The Salariya Book Company Ltd**
25 Marlborough Place, Brighton BN1 1UB
www.salariya.com

PB ISBN: 978-1-912537-57-0

SCRIBO BOOK HOUSE SCRIBBLERS

3 5 7 9 8 6 4 2

A CIP catalogue record for this book is available from the British Library.
Printed and bound in China.
Reprinted in MMXIX.

Visit
www.salariya.com
for our online catalogue and **free** fun stuff.

PAPER FROM

SUSTAINABLE
FORESTS

THE ART OF DRAWING
MANGA™

GIRLS & BOYS

BOOK HOUSE
a SALARIYA *imprint*

MAX MARLBOROUGH   DAVID ANTRAM

Contents

Characters

Making a start

Introduction

The key to drawing well is learning to look carefully. Study your subject until you know it really well. Keep a sketchbook with you and draw whenever you get the chance. Even doodling is good – it helps to make your drawing more confident. You'll soon develop your own style of drawing, but this book will help you to find your way.

Quick sketches

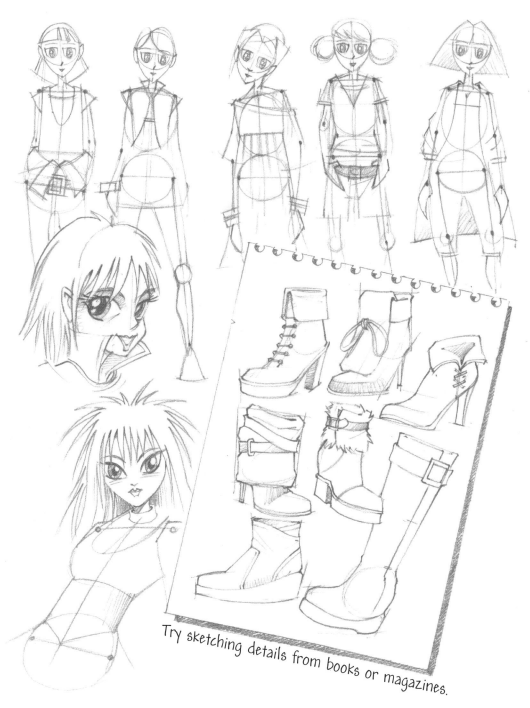

Try sketching details from books or magazines.

Introduction (2)

Practise drawing stick figures for basic poses...

...then dress them and add details.

It's important to experiment with different shapes and movements so that you gain experience. Look at examples of manga to see how other artists in the medium have handled the human form.

More quick sketches

Carry a sketchbook with you at all times so that you can use it if you see something that inspires you.

Perspective

Perspective is a way of drawing objects so that they look as though they have three dimensions. Note how the part that is closest to you looks larger, and the part furthest away from you looks smaller. That's just how things look in real life.

The vanishing point (V.P.) is the place in a perspective drawing where parallel lines appear to meet. The position of the vanishing point depends on the viewer's eye level.

V.P.

V.P. = vanishing point

Two-point perspective drawing

Two-point perspective uses two vanishing points: one for lines running along the length of the subject, and one on the opposite side for lines running across the width of the subject.

In this drawing the vanishing points are low. This gives the impression that you are looking up at the figure – very dramatic!

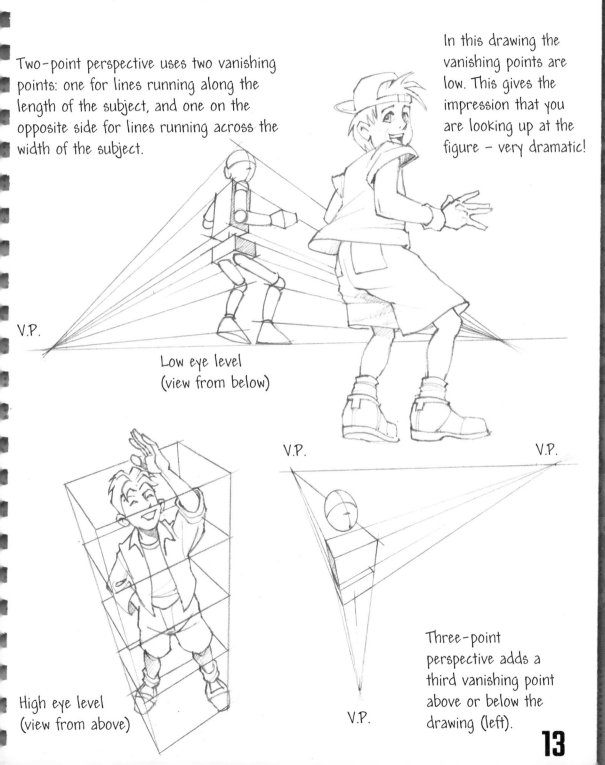

V.P.

Low eye level
(view from below)

V.P.

V.P.

High eye level
(view from above)

V.P.

Three-point perspective adds a third vanishing point above or below the drawing (left).

Materials

Pencils
Try out different grades of pencils. Hard pencils make fine grey lines and soft pencils make softer, darker marks.

Erasers
are useful for cleaning up drawings and removing construction lines.

Paper
Bristol paper is good for crayons, pastels and felt-tip pens. Watercolour paper is thicker; it is the best choice for water-based paints or inks.

Remember, the best equipment and materials will not necessarily make the best drawing – only practise will.

Use this sandpaper block if you want to shape your pencil to a really sharp point.

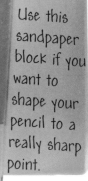

Inks
Use coloured inks straight from the bottle or dilute them with water.

Felt-tip pens
Felt-tips usually come in sets of mixed colours. The ones that make very thin lines are called fineliners.

Ink

Mixing palette

Fineliners

Dip-in pen nibs

Brushes

Correction fluid

Gouache

Technical drawing pens

Watercolours

Paints
Ordinary watercolours are translucent (see-through); gouache is not. Try other kinds of paints, too.

Pens
Technical drawing pens have cartridges which can be refilled or replaced. Old-fashioned dip-in pens are much cheaper and come in many different styles and sizes.

15

Styles

Try different types of drawing papers and materials. Experiment with pens, from felt-tips to ballpoints. They will make interesting marks. What happens if you draw with pen and ink on wet paper?

Silhouette
is a style of drawing which mainly relies on solid dark shapes.

Felt-tips

come in a range of line widths. The wider pens are good for filling in large areas of flat tone.

17

Styles continued

Pencil

drawings can include a vast amount of
detail and tone. Try different grades
of pencil to get a range of light and
shade effects in your drawings.

Lines drawn in **ink** cannot be erased, so unless you are very confident you may want to sketch your drawing in pencil first.

It can be tricky adding light and shade to a drawing with a pen. Use a solid layer of ink for the very darkest areas and cross-hatching (straight lines criss-crossing each other) for ordinary dark tones. Use hatching (straight lines running parallel to each other) for midtones.

Hatching

Cross-hatching

Body proportions

Heads in manga are drawn slightly bigger than in real life. Legs and hips make up more than half the overall height of the figure.

Proportions of a female character:

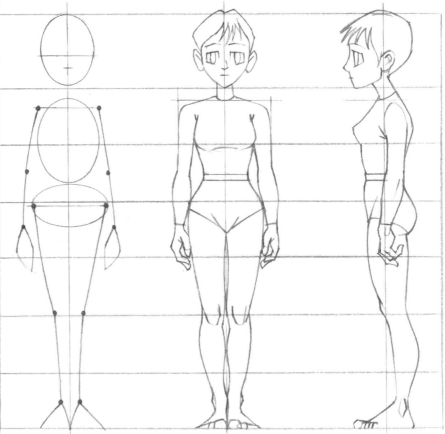

The eye level is about midway down the head.

Shoulders

Hips

Knees

Feet

Standing straight

Drawing a stick figure is the simplest way to make decisions about a pose. It helps you see how different positions can change the centre of balance.

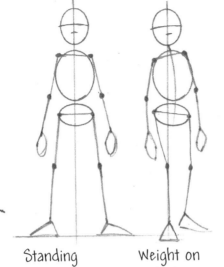

Standing straight

Weight on right leg

Weight on left leg

Centre of balance

Proportions of a male character:

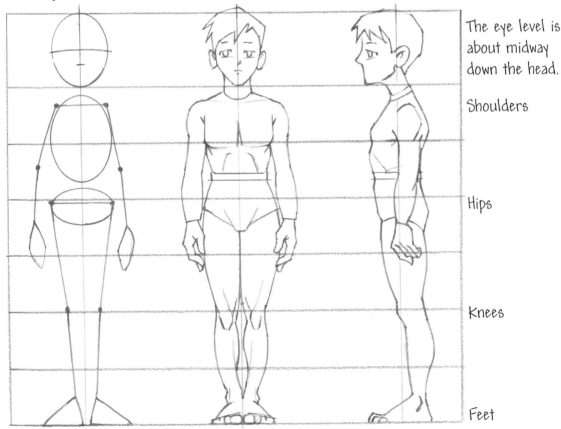

The eye level is about midway down the head.

Shoulders

Hips

Knees

Feet

Standing straight

Inking

Here's one way of inking over your final pencil drawing. Different tones of ink can be used to add depth to the drawing. Mix ink with water to achieve the tones you need.

Refillable inking pens come in various tip sizes. The tip is what determines the width of the line that is drawn. Sizes include: 0.1, 0.5, 1.0, 2.0 mm.

Correction fluid usually comes in small bottles or in pen format. This can be useful for cleaning up ink lines.

Here's one way of inking over your final pencil drawing.

Different tones of ink can be used to add depth to the drawing. Mix ink with water to achieve the tones you need.

Heads

Manga heads have a distinctive style and shape. Drawing different facial expressions is very important – it shows instantly what your character is thinking or feeling.

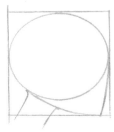

1. Start by drawing a square. Fit the head, chin and neck inside it to keep the correct proportions.

2. Draw two construction lines to position the top of the ear and the base of the nose.

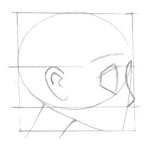

3. Add an oversized manga-style eye.

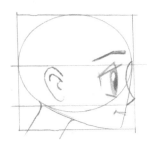

4. Add a pupil to the eye and draw the mouth.

5. Draw some manga-style hair.

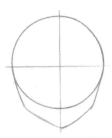

1. Draw a circle. Add construction lines through its centre point.

2. Using the construction lines, position the eyes, ears and mouth.

3. Add details.

4. Draw the hair.

Male character

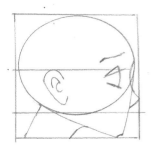

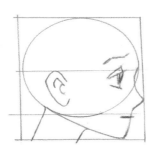

1. Add an oversized manga-style eye.

2. Add a pupil to the eye and draw the mouth.

3. Draw some manga-style hair.

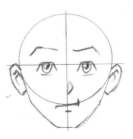

1. Draw a circle. Add construction lines through its centre point.

2. Using the construction lines, position the eyes, ears and mouth.

3. Draw the hair and add finishing touches.

Practise drawing heads from different angles.

Centre line

25

Heads continued

Practise drawing heads with different facial expressions.

Youth

Female

Male

Practising different facial expressions allows you to explore the personality of your character.

Dreamy

Centreline

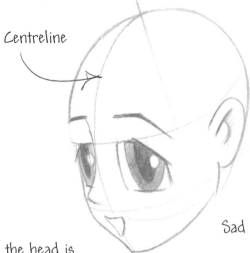

Sad

Whichever way the head is turned, the nose and mouth always stay on the centreline.

Surprised

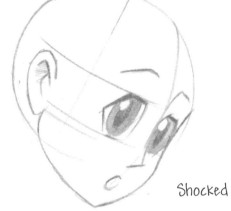

Shocked

Curious

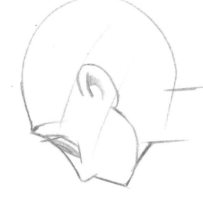

Fascinated

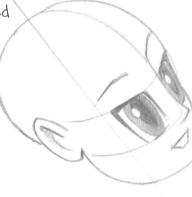

Male heads, by contrast, have thicker necks and a squared-off, chiselled jawline. They also have slightly smaller eyes than females and wider mouths.

Creases and folds

Clothes fall into natural creases and folds when worn. Look at real people to see how fabric drapes and how it falls into creases. This will help you to dress your characters more realistically.

These trousers have creased because the knees are bent. Excess fabric has gathered in folds and creases over the shoes.

Drawing from life can help you understand where and why creases and folds occur.

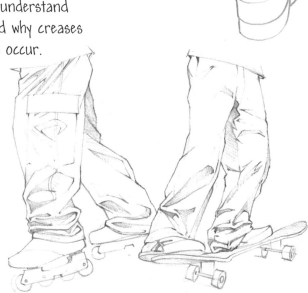

The way fabric is drawn can instantly give a sense of movement and action to a pose.

Shading clothes is also very important. Think of all the places the light won't reach, such as inside trouser legs.

Shading in pencil first before adding ink helps avoid mistakes.

Characters

Neko girl

Neko is Japanese for 'cat'. This character has catlike ears and a tail on an otherwise human body.

Cat ears

3. Draw stick arms and legs, with dots where the joints are. Add outline shapes for hands and feet.

These little circles are to remind you where the elbows and knees go.

1. Draw ovals for the head, body and hips. Add centre lines to divide the head vertically and horizontally. These will help you to place the ears and the nose.

2. Add lines for the spine and the angle of the hips and shoulders.

4. Sketch the teddy bear in the same way.

5. Using the construction lines as a guide, start to build up the main shapes and features.

Jagged hairline

Shadow

Big pupils

Pussycat bow

6. Draw the clothes, hair and facial features. This is where your drawing really starts to come to life.

meow

Why not add a catlike sound effect?

7. If you don't want your construction lines to show, erase them before you do the final shading and details.

8. Now finish all the little details such as the shading on the hair and shoes, and the pattern on the skirt and socks. Don't rush! The more carefully you do these finishing touches, the better your drawing will look.

33

Skateboarder

This young boy is a fantastic skateboarder. He can perform all sorts of amazing tricks and jumps at fast speeds.

1. Draw ovals for the head, body and hips. Add centre lines to divide the head vertically and horizontally. These will help you to place the ears and the nose.

2. Add lines for the spine and the angle of the hips and shoulders. Draw stick arms and legs, with dots where the joints are. Add outline shapes for hands and feet.

Start adding in the facial features and hair.

3. Using the construction lines as a guide, add the basic shapes of the body and clothes.

4. Add the basic shape of the skateboard.

These little circles are to remind you where the elbows and knees go.

5. Draw the clothes, hair and facial features. This is where your drawing really starts to come to life.

6. If you don't want your construction lines to show, erase them before you do the final shading and details.

Add the basic shape of the shirt.

Add dark shading to any area light wouldn't reach.

7. Now finish all the little details, such as the details of the clothes, hair and face, and the shading. Don't rush! The more carefully you do these finishing touches, the better your drawing will look.

Instead of shading your drawing you can try finishing your drawing in ink. Go over all outlines in ink and remove any pencil lines.

Schoolboy

This boy is dressed in a traditional Japanese school uniform called the gakuran.

1. Draw a circle for the head and ovals for the body and hips.

2. Add lines for the spine and the angle of the hips and shoulders.

3. Draw stick arms and legs with dots for the joints, and shapes for the hands and feet.

4. Use your guidelines to sketch in the neck, facial features and hair.

5. Using the construction lines as a guide, start drawing in the main shapes of the body.

Small circles indicate the positions of elbows and knees.

6. Now start to sketch out the final shapes of clothes, hair, arms and legs.

7. If you don't want your construction lines to show, erase them carefully before you add the finishing touches: shading, facial features, patterns on the clothes.

8. Complete your drawing adding all the final detail.

Look at how angles in the body create folds in the fabric of the clothes.

Add details to the bag and strap.

Add shading to any areas light wouldn't reach.

If you want a different final look to your drawing you can try finishing it in ink. Carefully go over any outlines and then remove any leftover pencil lines with an eraser.

High-class girl

This character may behave like a spoiled brat. She has the pride and social standing of a girl from a privileged background. She can be extremely bad-tempered and sometimes feels lonely.

1. Draw a circle for the head and ovals for the body and hips.

2. Add lines for the spine and the angle of the hips and shoulders.

3. Draw stick arms and legs with dots for the joints.

4. Use your guidelines to sketch in the neck and facial features.

Small circles indicate the positions of elbows and knees.

5. Using the construction lines as a guide, start drawing in the main shapes of the body.

Lengthen the legs to give a more dramatic perspective – just like fashion designers do!

6. Now start to sketch out the final shapes of clothes, hair, arms and legs.

Dramatic hair

Highlights in the eyes help to bring the face to life.

Even slim legs like these need some muscles!

7. If you don't want your construction lines to show, erase them carefully before you add the finishing touches: shading, facial features, patterns on the clothes.

Otaku

An otaku is a person who follows their hobbies and interests to an obsessive level. This boy loves toy spaceships!

1. Draw ovals for the head, body and hips.

2. Add lines for the spine and the angle of the shoulders and hips.

3. Sketch the basic shape of a spaceship.

Add some more detail to the spaceship.

4. Draw stick arms with dots for the joints and shapes for the hands.

5. Using your construction lines, sketch in the facial features and hair shape.

6. Draw in the basic shapes of the body using the construction lines as a guide. Draw small circles for the joints.

Add some strands of hair.

7. Draw in the details of the clothes and facial expression.

8. Erase your construction lines if you don't want them to show.

Add more technical detail to the spaceship.

Leave the lenses of the glasses blank to suggest a reflective surface.

9. Complete your drawing, adding final details and shading where necessary.

You could try finishing your drawing in ink.

41

Shy girl

The shy girl enjoys reading (especially horror!) and dreams of becoming a writer.

1. Draw circles for the head and hips and an oval for the body.

2. Add lines for the spine and the angle of the hips and shoulders.

4. Using your construction lines, add the neck and sketch in the facial features.

3. Draw stick arms and legs with dots for the joints.

Remember to draw both legs, even though one is almost hidden from view.

5. Flesh out the arms and legs, using circles to indicate elbows and knees.

7. Erase your construction lines if you don't want them to show.

8. Take plenty of time to finish the details of the face and hair, the laced bodice and the fringed skirt.

6. Draw the shapes of the billowing skirt, the boots, bodice and hair.

Heavy fringe

Flowing hair

Note how the long gloves crease at the elbows.

Shading shows which leg is in front and which one is behind.

Long, elegant fingers help to give her character.

Eyes

Draw the eye shape and then add the pupil.

Either leave the highlights white, or paint them white using gouache or correcting fluid.

Highlight

Magical girl

This girl may possess superhuman abilities and often has a secret identity. She fights evil and protects the Earth.

1. Draw different-sized ovals for the head, body and hips.

Lines and small circles show the positions of the fingers.

2. Add a line for the spine and others to show the angle of the hips and shoulders.

3. Draw stick arms and legs with dots for the joints and outline shapes for the hands and feet.

4. Using your construction lines as a guide, draw the main shapes of the body and the position of the facial features.

In this pose, the graceful positions of the hands and feet are particularly important. Get the basic shapes right before you move on to the details.

The position of the thumb is important.

5. This figure wears a traditional Japanese costume. Draw the sleeves and skirt of the kimono, using angular lines to create folds in the fabric. Draw the face and the fluttering hair.

Note the wide draped sleeves, the collar, and the decorative sash and bow.

Try to get nice flowing lines in the hair.

Although the legs are hidden, the kimono is shaped by them.

6. Erase the construction lines if you want to, then draw the draped folds and tucks in the costume. Finish off all remaining costume details and add shading.

The girl's legs bend slightly at the hips and knees. The shadow on the skirt is an effective way to show this.

Bosozoku leader

Bosozoku is the name given to motorcycle gangs in Japan. This leader carries a Rising Sun flag and is ready for action.

1. Draw different-sized ovals for the head, body and hips.

2. Add lines for the spine and to show the angle of the hips and shoulders.

Draw a line for the flagpole.

3. Draw stick arms with dots for the joints and outline shapes for the hands.

Bandana

The hand is gripping the flagpole.

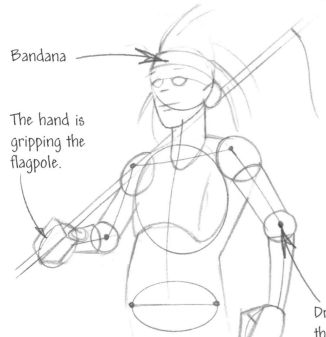

4. Using your construction lines as a guide, draw the main shapes of the body and the positions of the facial features.

Draw circles for the elbow and shoulder joints.

5. Add detail to the face, hair and costume.

6. Erase the construction lines if you want to. Finish off all remaining costume details and add shading.

Start to add shade to the darkest areas.

Shade in the flag design.

Add the fingers.

Add creases and folds to the fabric.

Draw in the leather glove details.

Go over the main outlines in ink and then erase the pencil drawing underneath for a different outcome.

Baseball star

This baseball star is the captain of his school team. His dream is to win the Summer Koshien – the nationwide school baseball championship.

1. Draw ovals for the head, body and hips.

Add a line for the bat.

2. Add lines for the spine and the angle of the shoulders and hips.

3. Draw stick arms with dots for the joints and shapes for the hands and feet.

The wide legs in this pose give a sense of action.

Sketch in basic facial features and a hat.

4. Draw in tube-shaped arms and legs with circles for the knees and elbows.

Draw in the basic shape of the bat.

Don't forget to use your construction lines as a guide when drawing the basic shapes of the body.

5. Start to add detail to the face, body and clothes.

Add the hat and hair.

Draw in the fingers of the hand gripping the bat.

Draw in lines for the folds in the clothes.

6. Erase the construction lines if you want to.

7. Complete the drawing adding all final details and important shading.

Add shade to areas light wouldn't reach.

The folds and creases in the fabric show how the body is twisting.

You can try finishing your drawing in ink.

Draw in your own baseball gear details.

49

Cheery girl

The cheery girl is easygoing and lives alone. She enjoys her privacy, yet she makes friends with absolutely anyone.

I. This time you have the challenge of drawing two figures together! Draw the different-sized ovals and the other construction lines in the usual way. Notice how the backs of the two girls touch.

Notice that the overall shape of the two figures makes a triangle or pyramid.

Note how all the feet are at different angles.

2. Draw in tube-shaped arms and legs with circles for the knees and elbows.

3. Position the facial features.

Don't forget to use your construction lines as a guide when drawing the basic shapes of the body.

Jagged hairline

4. Now sketch in the basic shapes of the clothes and the facial features. Note how the perky girl's hand rests on her forehead and how her arm passes in front of her friend's body. Draw the scarves with curved lines so they look as though they wrap around the girls' necks.

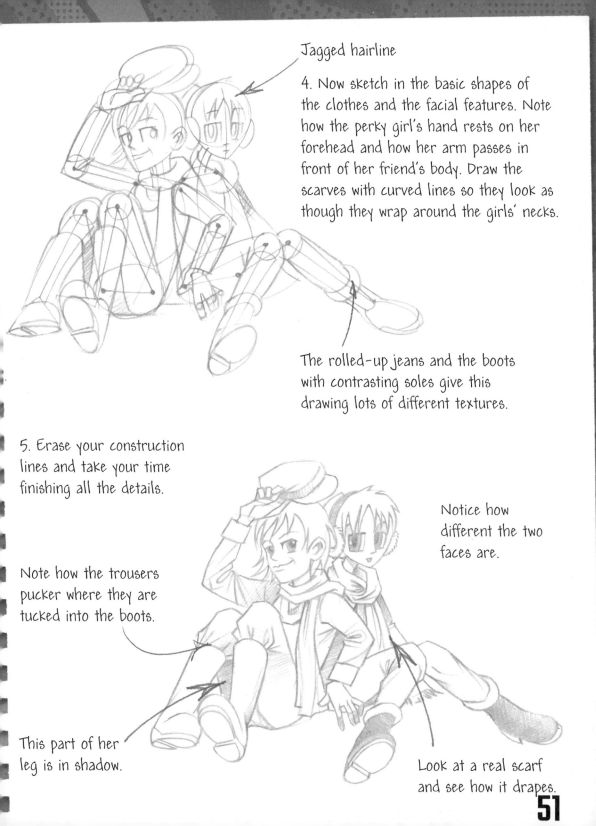

The rolled-up jeans and the boots with contrasting soles give this drawing lots of different textures.

5. Erase your construction lines and take your time finishing all the details.

Notice how different the two faces are.

Note how the trousers pucker where they are tucked into the boots.

This part of her leg is in shadow.

Look at a real scarf and see how it drapes.

Festival boy

This boy is ready for the New Year's festival, wearing a traditional outfit.

1. Draw ovals for the head, body and hips.

2. Add lines for the spine and to show the angle of the hips and shoulders.

3. Draw stick arms with dots for the joints and shapes for the hands.

Add a line for the baton.

4. Draw in tube-shaped arms and legs with circles for the knees and elbows.

Add the darkest area of shade.

Small circles indicate the positions of elbows and knees.

5. Start to add detail to the face, body and hands.

Draw two white paper streams (shide) coming off the baton.

6. Add more detail to the face and hands, then draw in the clothes around the body.

Short spiky hairstyle.

7. Erase the construction lines if you want to. Finish off all remaining costume details and add shading.

Pay particular attention to the folds and creases of the traditional outfit, taking care to see how they affect the shading.

Here's the same drawing finished in ink.

Stylish girl

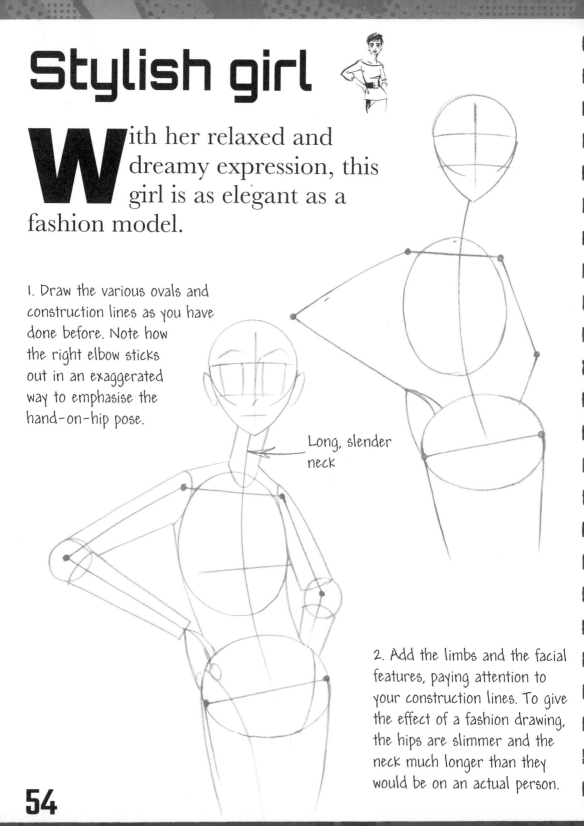

With her relaxed and dreamy expression, this girl is as elegant as a fashion model.

1. Draw the various ovals and construction lines as you have done before. Note how the right elbow sticks out in an exaggerated way to emphasise the hand-on-hip pose.

Long, slender neck

2. Add the limbs and the facial features, paying attention to your construction lines. To give the effect of a fashion drawing, the hips are slimmer and the neck much longer than they would be on an actual person.

3. Start drawing the details, such as the sleeves and neckline of the fashion top. Draw the belt and the hem of the top with curved lines so that they appear to go around the body.

Short, spiky hairstyle.

Enlarging the pupils of the eyes adds to the relaxed look of the dreamy girl.

Eyes with large pupils and highlights

Collarbone

Fabric creases at the elbow.

4. Erase construction lines before adding final details such as the folds and puckers in the girl's top.

5. Here's the same drawing finished with brush and ink. This style is often used for illustrations in fashion magazines. Decide which lines you want to ink in before you make any brushmarks.

Geeky girl

This girl's a bit of a tomboy, and is given to making unembarrassed naughty comments. She can be a worrying presence for those around her.

1. Draw the basic ovals and construction lines as usual. Try to get as much contrast as possible between the poses of the shy girl and her more confident friend.

The elegant shapes of the fingers are especially important.

2. Sketch the arms and legs and the main facial features. Note how the two heads face in different directions: one is in profile (side view) and the other is turned partly towards the viewer. Contrasts like this make a picture much more interesting – and lifelike.

3. Draw the details of the clothes and shoes. Try to get lively, swinging shapes in the hair.

We are going to finish this drawing in silhouette, so concentrate on details that will help to make the outline more interesting, such as the fringe, ponytail, fingers and shoelaces.

4. Silhouette is a very effective style. It looks easy, but to make a silhouette work all the small details of the drawing need to be thought out carefully before applying the ink.

Details such as the belt, the sandal straps and the tops of the socks can be left white.

Boy detective

The boy detective can follow the tiniest of clues to solve the most complex of puzzles.

1. Draw ovals for the head, body and hips.

Divide the head using construction lines.

2. Add lines for the spine and the angle of the shoulders and hips.

Add a line for the magnifying glass.

Add the basic facial features and a hat.

Add the oval magnifying lens.

3. Draw stick arms with dots for the joints and shapes for the hands and feet.

4. Draw in tube-shaped arms and legs with circles for the knees and elbows.

Draw in the shape of the fingers.

Add the hair.

5. Add more detail to the face and hands, then draw in the clothes around the body.

Draw in the fingers.

6. Erase the construction lines if you want to. Finish off all remaining costume details and add shading.

Add shade to areas light wouldn't reach.

Add detail to the shoes.

Add folds and creases to the coat and shorts.

You can try finishing your drawing in ink.

Glossary

Baton A thin stick that can be carried and twirled in the air during a performance.

Bodice A sleeveless undergarment worn by a woman, usually laced up at the front.

Composition The positioning of the various parts of a picture on the drawing paper.

Construction lines Guidelines used in the early stages of a drawing which are usually erased later.

Cross-hatching A series of criss-crossing lines used to add shade to a drawing.

Hatching A series of parallel lines used to add shade to a drawing.

Kimono A robe-like, traditional Japanese item of clothing.

Magnifying glass An implement that can be used to study small details in objects by making them appear bigger.

Manga A Japanese word for 'comic' or 'cartoon'; also the style of drawing that is used in Japanese comics.

Neko The Japanese word for 'cat'; also a manga character that is part-human, part-cat.

Obsessive Having a passionate interest in something to a degree that might be considered excessive.

Privileged Having certain rights and advantages that others do not.

Proportions The size of each part of something in relation to the whole.

Pupils The tiny holes in the middle of a person's eyes through which light passes, allowing them to see the world.

Sash A strip of cloth worn around the waist or over the shoulder, usually as part of a uniform.

Silhouette A drawing that shows only a dark shape, like a shadow, sometimes with a few details left white.

Three-dimensional Having an effect of depth, so as to look like a real character rather than a flat picture.

Tone The contrast between light and shade that helps to add depth to a picture.

Vanishing point The place in a perspective drawing where parallel lines appear to meet.

Index